Simple Fool Proof Ways to Cut Your Rate, Limit Your Risk, and Skyrocket Your Cash Flow in Commercial Real Estate

Insider Tells All: Exposing Dirty Little Secrets that 99% of ALL INVESTORS DON'T KNOW ABOUT

Charles L Knighton II, MSRE

Copyright © 2019 by Charles Knighton II, MSRE

All rights reserved. No part of this publication may be reproduced, distributed, or transmitted in any form or by any means, including photocopying, recording, or other electronic or mechanical methods, without the prior written permission of the publisher, except in the case of brief quotations embodied in critical reviews and certain other noncommercial uses permitted by copyright law. For permission requests, write to the publisher, addressed "Attention: Permissions Coordinator," at the email address below.

Charles L Knighton II, MSRE
CREBook2019@gmail.com

Ordering Information: Quantity sales. Special discounts are available on quantity purchases by corporations, associations, and others. For details, contact the publisher at the email address above.

Printed in the United States of America

Publisher's Cataloging-in-Publication data
Knighton II, Charles.
A title of a book : "Simple Fool Proof Ways to Cut Your Rate, Limit Your Risk, and Skyrocket Your Cash Flow in Commercial Real Estate"/ Charles Knighton II, MSRE
ISBN-13: 978-1098619572

Second Edition

14 13 12 11 10 / 10 9 8 7 6 5 4 3 2 1

INTRODUCTION

My name is Charles Knighton II, a Multifamily Loan Advisor specializing in placing long term fixed rate debt on multifamily investment property across the country. I help investors get access to the best funding for their multifamily investment: fast access to capital, best terms, and no surprises that may hinder their opportunity for a great return.

I started in real estate like most people, not knowing much about real estate investing but being very intrigued by it. I heard about the Donald Trumps, Robert Kiyosokis, and Robert Allens of the world and wanted to be like them. I begin investing in residential property and duplexes part-time in 2005. After the market crashed, I decided to venture into commercial real estate property, as I saw an opportunity to acquire property at a huge discount. Unfortunately, I didn't know much about cap rates, net operating incomes, or debt service coverage ratios. I was lending on the expertise of my partner, an experienced commercial investor, and my mentor, a real estate hedge fund manager with over $600M in assets under management. A year later, after putting our largest multifamily portfolio under contract only to have it fall through due to a lack of fully understanding the ins and outs of the deal, my partner passed away from a stomach aneurysm leaving me to venture into commercial real estate on my own. Because I had just a small amount of experience in commercial real estate and multifamily finance, my mentor recommended that I obtain a master's degree in commercial real estate finance. Since obtaining an MSRE, I've worked at numerous corporations both large and small, sharpening my finance skills and developing new ones. Being both a commercial real estate lender and a capital markets advisor – where I helped many investors achieve *maximum financing, I've learned how to get deals done, how to achieve maximum debt terms, and how to beat the bank at its own game by making subtle changes to your annual operations to increase profitability and lower risk.*

Although many people could benefit greatly from reading this book, I specifically wrote "Simple Foolproof Ways to Cut Your Rate, Limit Your Risk, and Skyrocket Your Cash Flow in Commercial Real Estate" for the professional commercial real estate and multifamily investor or third party who works with these types of investors, who own one or more commercial and multifamily properties valued between $1,000,000 to $10,000,000 and who has a balloon payment coming due or are looking to quickly add value to their property in the next 12-18 months. These investors have a decision to make now; do they sell or do they refinance. Being a Multifamily Loan Advisor, I've assisted many of my clients in making this decision, and I'd like to help you do the same; that's why I wrote this book.

On the other hand, if you're absolutely brand new to real estate, or an institutional investor who purchases $50M+ property, then this book may not be for you. However, you will still get something from it. If you're extremely new, I've included a glossary at the back of the book for your review which may help you understand some of the concepts mentioned in the chapters ahead.

I have broken this book up in two sections: The "What" and The "How". The "What" section of this book describes what certain terms are, what are basic ways to understand how lenders view transactions, what can you do to improve your chances of achieving maximum leverage, and understanding what interest rates are and how they are set. The "How" section of this book describes how to underwrite to a maximum value, how to increase your cash flow, how to lower your rate, how to combine your documents in a lender friendly manner, and how to automate this process.

In this book, you will learn:

1. *How to Structure Your Asset for Maximum Profitability*
2. *How to Cut Your Interest Rate to the Lowest Possible in the Marketplace*
3. *How to Skyrocket Your Cash Flow Using Concepts 99% of Commercial Real Estate Investors Know Nothing About*

Without any further ado, let's get started...

TABLE OF CONTENTS

INTRODUCTION 3
TABLE OF CONTENTS 6
Section I
Is My Deal Financeable? If So, What Do I Need To Know In Order To Position My Property As Financeable? 7
CHAPTER ONE Is Your Property Structured For Maximum Profitability? 10
CHAPTER TWO What You Can Do to Achieve Maximum Cash Flow 23
CHAPTER THREE What to Do to Get the Best and Lowest Interest Rate Available? 33
Section II
How to Get Your Deal Financed With Max Cash Flow and the Lowest Rate Guaranteed! How Do You Find the Best Lender For Your Situation? 40
CHAPTER FOUR Underwriting the Lender Way for Maximum Profitability 44
CHAPTER FIVE Three Questions You Never Ask That Can Add Over $1,000,000 in Current Value to Your Property 55
CHAPTER SIX How to Negotiate Max Leverage While Also Achieving a Positive Cash-on-Cash Return 60
CHAPTER SEVEN How to Use an Owner Occupied Trick to Get You Higher Leverage and the Lowest Possible Rate When Acquiring Your Next Property 69
CHAPTER EIGHT What is a Financing Memorandum and Why Do You Need One? 73
CHAPTER NINE A Property Zoning Report? What is This and Why is It So Important to Have? 79
CHAPTER TEN This Process Seems Very Complicated and Overwhelming. Can Someone Do This For Me? 84
APPENDIX: 88

Section I

Is My Deal Financeable? If So, What Do I Need To Know In Order To Position My Property As Financeable?

As I mentioned in the introduction to this book, I will be separating the information into two Sections, the first is very general – the "What" to know; the second is the "How" to do.

In this section, we will discuss "What" you need to know in order to position your property for maximum profitability. This is very important to understand. Please keep in mind, although the information in this section may seem easily comprehensible, it can be very difficult to implement. Not because these are hard tasks to move forward with, but because it infringes on the old-school ways of understanding commercial real estate finance. In the numerous transactions that I've been involved in, I have never had a client that did not need to implement something new into their property in order to maximize its financeability. It's like the old adage "You can't teach an old dog new tricks". Well I intend to at least introduce new tricks for the old dog to consider. This will cause you to think differently about your asset.

In the coming chapters, we will be discussing the following:

- ***What do You Have to do to Structure Your Property for Maximum Value***
    - This will help you manage your risk. Knowing how to structure your deal for maximum profitability will ensure you ALWAYS have value in your property and you will NEVER be underwater, regardless of

what the market does,
- **What Does It Mean to Achieve Maximum Cash Flow**
    - Understanding how to calculate Cash Flow will help you understand what you need to do to SKYROCKET IT,
- **What is an Interest Rate and How are They Set?**
    - If you understand what interest rates are, how they are set, and what part of the interest rate is negotiable, then you can CUT YOUR current INTEREST RATE or refinance to obtain a lower interest rate!

Before we get into the "What" section of this book, let's discuss what it means to have a financeable deal. A financeable deal is one that without considering any other factors, your property, its location, its lease structure, and overall feasibility [economically, functionality, physically] would be acceptable for a lender to finance it. To determine if your property meets these criteria, you'd have to ask yourself a couple questions. What property type do you have? What's the asset class? Where is the property located?

There are many factors to consider in regard to knowing if you have a financeable asset; underwriting your product, underwriting your loan, looking at your situation in its entirety, etc. As an example, let's say you visit your local community bank, and your local commercial lender says, "You know what? I can finance your $2 million dollar multi-tenant retail building. I can provide you with a term sheet that states we can give you up to 70% leverage (or loan to value), a 4.5% interest rate with a 25-year amortization, and a five-year loan term." Here's the problem with that. Most investors would hold that lender *accountable for the terms on that term sheet if, during the underwriting process, the lender comes back to you and says "Sorry, after reviewing all the pertinent information about your asset, I can only offer you 65% leverage, a three-year loan term, a 4.75% interest rate, and a 20-year amortization". How would you feel? Terrible, right? Well, unfortunately, you put yourself in that situation. This is the NUMBER ONE mistake I see when working with investors. Understanding why the lender had to change their offering will help you not only be aware of the reason, but also know what to do so you can avoid going through this.*

You'd want to make sure the lender has seen your property, underwritten your property, and have taken a look at your complete financial picture before providing you with terms. Another thing to consider is – how will this loan affect your investment objective? You have to start every loan query off with an overall objection. To an owner who wants to own multiple properties and retire on the cash flow, a 20-year amortization may sound good, but a 25-year amortization would be even better, as a 25-year amortization could allow you to increase your cash flow. We will discuss more about how your objective plays a part in financing in Section 2.

Let's start with structuring your property for maximum profitability.

CHAPTER ONE

Is Your Property Structured For Maximum Profitability?

During the Great Recession and its aftermath, many commercial values were hit hard, as the cap rates increased almost 200 basis points or 2%! To be sure we're on the same page, commercial values are determined by dividing the net operating income (NOI) of an income-producing property by a percentage known as a capitalization rate (cap rate). The cap rate is found by dividing the net operating income (NOI) of an income-producing property by its purchase price or market value. The cap rate measures the relative risk of a real estate investment stream. This is very important so I'm mentioning it again – the cap rate measures the relative risk of a real estate investment stream. In other words, the higher the cap rate, the higher the risk. This percentage rate also determines what the value of your property is or what the purchase price could be. As an example, let's say you have a mobile home park that has an NOI of $100,000 per year. In general, mobile home parks are perceived to be riskier than other assets, so let's give it a 10% cap rate. This would equate to a property value of $1,000,000. Now during the 18 months of the Great Recession, the cap rates increased 2%, or in this example, to 12%. What did this do to the value of our example mobile home park property? If the net operating income did not change, the property would have decreased in value about $166,000! Wow! What a disappointment!

Why Does This Matter?

Not only is structuring your property for maximum profitability important if economic turmoil strikes, but it's also important if you want to limit your risk and either obtain the highest possible value for your property if you decide to sell it, or the highest proceeds if you decide to refinance your asset to pull cash out. If you own a property type other than multifamily, you'd want to make sure you have solid tenants with strong leases in a good location. If you're looking to sell your asset, and you add value to the property, you'd have to support the value you've added by providing documentation proving the changes you've made.

If you plan to acquire a property then sell it relatively quickly, obtaining the necessary financing to acquire the property would take different loan terms and options. As an example, if you wanted to rehab and flip a property, then you might not want to lock yourself into a 10-year loan with an expensive prepayment penalty. Or, let's say you wanted to potentially keep this property in your retirement portfolio; you may consider locking in the lowest interest rate possible for the longest term. In moving ahead in this chapter, let's assume you intend to keep your property in your retirement portfolio and want to increase the value to partially liquidate your equity by refinancing.

What Are the Primary Lease Types and Which Lease Type is Best for Financing Commercial Real Estate Investment Property?

When I speak about lease structures, I am only speaking about the lease type, not including clauses or various lease interests that the landlord may include in specific leases. Most of these lease structures are typically found in commercial real estate property types, not in multifamily. Please keep in mind that certain lease terminology may infer something different in your market than in another. Also, the expenses that are included in a lease from your market may be different from a lease that may be written in another. Because of this, I will be fairly general.

There are three primary lease types in a commercial real estate transaction; a gross lease, a net lease, and a modified gross lease.

A gross lease is when the tenant pays for the base rent and no landlord expenses. Although gross leases tend to have higher base rents in relation to the other leases, the property may not be positioned to achieve the highest value. This is also considered a traditional lease because the landlord usually builds the cost of taxes, insurance, and common area maintenance (CAM) into the rent. This is typically how residential or multifamily leases are structured. Because the landlord takes care of all the expenses that this tenant incurs -- i.e., the electric, water, taxes, insurance, common area maintenance -- lenders tend to look at these lease structures as less favorable than a net lease structure.

A net lease is when the tenant pays a base rent but also takes care of some or all the landlord's expenses depending on which net lease structure the tenant and landlord have negotiated. Within the net lease family is a single net, a double net, and a triple net lease.

A single net lease is when the tenant pays a base rent and is also responsible for a pro rata share of the overall taxes. The landlord is responsible for every other expense the property incurs. As an example, if a tenant occupies 50% of the total space of a building and the taxes incurred were $10,000 for the year, the tenant would be responsible for paying $5,000 towards the expenses. You will hardly ever see this lease type. Not only is this a risky lease for the lender, but the landlord may lose autonomy over making sure the taxes are paid on time.

A double net lease (also referred to as an NN lease) is when the tenant pays a base rent in addition to the pro rata share of its taxes and insurance. The landlord would still be responsible for taking care of the CAM. In some transactions and locations, a property could also fall under the double net category if all the property's expenses (CAM, taxes, and insurance) are the responsibility of the tenant, BUT the landlord is responsible for roof and structure. As an example, Mattress Firm and Dunkin' Donut properties are usually on this type of double net lease structure.

A net-net-net lease (NNN), also known as a triple net lease, is when the tenant pays a base rent in addition to the common area maintenance (CAM), the taxes, and the insurance. In some transactions and depending on your location, even if the roof and structure is not taken care of by the tenant, the lease is considered a triple net lease because the insurance, taxes, and the CAM are not the responsibility of the landlord. To clarify, many investors have come across the term "absolute triple net" or "absolute net" which takes all the responsibility of managing the property from the landlord and puts them on the tenant's shoulders. The rents on a property that has this lease structure may be lower, as the landlord will inevitably receive net income. This is the preferred structure for investors who are looking to park their money into a property and potentially retire. Lenders[1] also prefer leases to be set up in this manner if the investor is located miles away from the property or if the investor has little to no experience managing commercial real estate. An absolute triple net lease structure is considered the most favorable lease structure to lenders and to buyers in the marketplace.

The third lease type is called a modified gross lease. A modified gross lease is when the tenant is responsible for a base rent but also a portion of the expenses. They may not have to take care of the full amount of the taxes, insurance, or CAM, but they are responsible for a small amount of them. The landlord and the tenant will basically share the expenses incurred by owning the property.

Out of the lease structures described above, which lease is best for your tenants? Well, as the investor, it would depend on your goals as it relates to this property. If you intend on self-managing the property, you may not be worried about the expenses as much as you would if the property is located in Florida and you live in California. If you are a hands-on manager, you could get a gross lease and decrease your expenses the best way you can. As an example, a previous client of mine owned an industrial complex where all of the tenants were on gross leases. The investor lived in the property's office so being a hands on manager was something that he was accustomed to. As an engineer who loved solar products, my client was able to use his knowledge of solar products to install solar energy panels on the roofs and around the industrial complex. Doing so allowed him to not only charge his tenants a high base rent, but also lower the costs of his electric and water expenses by over $10,000 per

---

[1] Please note, I will use "Lender" throughout this book interchangeably with commercial real estate lender, banker, or the bank/financing institution

year.

Now, if you're not a hands-on manager, don't kid yourself. Go for the double net or triple net lease. If you own the property and plan to sell it or refinance, you want to make sure you have NNN leases in place. Today, cap rates on triple net properties are on average at least 2% lower than a property with a double net lease structure. Like our $1,000,000 example, that's an additional $160,000 in value. This will ensure you receive the highest value on your sale, your lender will provide you with the highest possible cash-out proceeds – considering the appropriate debt coverage[2] is met, and you can make the most money from your property.

So what do I want you to take away from this?

If you are looking to maximize your value and pull cash out of your commercial real estate property or sell your asset to invest in another investment property, it might be a good idea to have your tenants on a triple net lease. Now, here's something to think about. If you can cash out with a high value or sell at a top price, how do you maximize your next investment? Well, with the cash, purchase another property with a gross lease structure and convert your leases to NNN to immediately increase your property's value.

How Do the Lease Terms Affect Value?

Another factor to consider is how long the leases are. This does not apply to multifamily properties due to the traditional nature of the leases. This will, however, apply to a multifamily property that has a master lease – discussed below. Most small commercial properties,

---

[2] Debt Service or DSCR from Chapter 2 *"This is calculated by dividing the annual Net Operating Income by the Annual Debt Service [NOI/ADS]. Many lenders in today's market need to see a debt coverage ratio of over 1.25x on multifamily and 1.30x on other property types."*

like office flex buildings or small multi-tenant retail buildings, have lease terms that range from three to five years. Keep in mind, the longer the lease term, the longer your loan term.

Risk is judged differently, depending on what type of lender is offering the debt. If you're working with a lender at a regional bank, they're going to take a different risk approach to lending on the transaction than a conduit lender, a credit union lender, or a life insurance company that lends on commercial real estate. Think about it like this: if you plan to refinance your property and go to a lender with tenants who are on month-to-month leases, will they look favorably or unfavorably on your property and its lease structure? Unfavorably, of course. If you want to satisfy the requirement of having a solid deal to present, you have to minimize the risk by extending your lease terms as long as possible.

In an appreciating market, most commercial real estate investors are putting their tenants on month-to-month leases. For example, a multifamily investor with tenants on month-to-month leases could benefit the investor because it allows the landlord to increase rents a few times during a year versus once per year. If the property is 100% occupied, a month-to-month tenant that is paying low rent could potentially be replaced that would allow the owner to release the units to the market and demand a higher rent. Also, if an investor owns a retail building, if a tenant is on a fixed month-to-month rental schedule and misses a lease payment, there's a clause that can be added to the lease that allows the owner to increase the rental rate every year on the property, if they wanted to. The owner/investor can also evict the tenant, then replace them with a stronger, more credit-worthy tenant and lock this new tenant in for five years. Keep in mind, if you lock a tenant in on a five-year lease, they're tied to *that amount for five years, unless you have rent bumps in the lease agreement.*

What I can tell you is that lenders do not like month-to-month lease agreements, so if you bring them a rent roll that says, "Hey, all my tenants are on month-to-month leases," they're going to shorten your loan term accordingly. Most lenders won't even give you a loan based on a month-to-month rent roll. They'll either tell you to extend your month-to-month leases to annual, or longer leases, or they won't even do the loan. So, if you're looking to get a loan with the lowest possible rate and the best possible terms, make sure you lock your tenants into a long-term lease.

Think about it like this: when a bank lends you 75% LTV on your asset, they are inevitably purchasing your property for 75% LTV. Can you imagine if you got a deal 75 cents on the dollar? It's still a risk, whether it's through an acquisition, or a refinance, it's still on a lender's balance sheet. You have to look at it as a risk. Mitigating that risk is what's important to getting your loan funded.

But What About Master Leases?

Master Leases are when there's one lease on a property with multiple units. Lenders will match the term of the loan to the master lease term. As an example, years ago a commercial real estate agent gave me a call to ask what lenders will do for a New York borrower who was interested in acquiring a multifamily property in Florida. The property was a newly developed, 60-unit multifamily property being leased to a local college on a master lease. Although there were 60 individual units at the location, the master lease was only for three years. Because of that, lenders in the market was only able to offer a three-year loan term. Now, if the units were leased out individually on an annual basis, a lender would be more than happy to provide a 10-year fixed rate loan. Isn't it funny how that works?

Do Tenants Matter When Trying to Sell My Property or Refinance It?

Let's talk about tenant mix. In the four major food groups, retail, industrial, apartment (multifamily), and office, you have different types of tenants. Let's look at the possible tenant structure in a multi-tenant retail building.

Tenants are categorized according to the size of their business, and their credit record. These tenants can either be national or credit, regional, local, non-credit, franchised, or destination tenants.

National (Credit)

National tenants usually have locations in most areas of the country and are rated by an agency such as Moody's or Standard & Poor's (S&P) and are usually publicly traded. One of the most common yardsticks is that they have yearly sales greater than $100 million and locations in multiple regions and states. Some tenants are considered credit if they have a nationwide presence with multiple locations and sales greater than $100 million but lack "bond-rated" credit. To a lender, a credit tenant has to have a BBB- rating or better. Some examples of credit tenants are Walgreens, CVS, AutoZone Corp, Big Lots, and JP Morgan Chase.

Investment Grade	'AAA'	Extremely strong capacity to meet financial commitments. Highest Rating.
	'AA'	Very strong capacity to meet financial commitments.
	'A'	Strong capacity to meet financial commitments but somewhat susceptible to adverse economic conditions and changes in circumstances.
	'BBB'	Adequate capacity to meet financial commitments, but more subject to adverse economic conditions.
	'BBB-'	Considered lowest investment grade by market participants.
Speculative Grade	'BB+'	Considered highest speculative grade by market participants.
	'BB'	Less vulnerable in the near-term but faces major ongoing uncertainties to adverse business, financial, and economic conditions.
	'B'	More vulnerable to adverse business, financial, and economic conditions but currently has the capacity to meet financial commitments.
	'CCC'	Currently vulnerable and dependent on favorable business, financial, and economic conditions but currently has the capacty to meet financial commitments
	'CC'	Currently highly vulnerable.
	'C'	Currently highly vulnerable obligations and other defined cicumstances.
	'D'	Payment default on financial commitments.

Regional

Regional tenants have multiple locations (at least 10 in a county or other geographical region) and minimum sales of $50 million. As with national tenants, the individual investors' definition of "regional" will vary.

Regional businesses are often owned and operated by an individual or a partnership. Some examples of a regional tenant is Publix Supermarkets, Amscot Financial Corporation, BJ's Restaurant, Inc.

Local

Local tenants usually have one to fifteen stores within a closely defined area. There's always a solid store in a shopping center or retail strip center that have a local tenant that everyone in your area knows. In Florida, as an example, there's Miami Subs & Grill Restaurants.

Non-credit

Non-credit tenants do not have a strong financial statement or multiple locations. This is the mom & pop restaurant, barbershop, or retail store.

Franchise

Many national businesses like Subway, KFC, or Burger King have franchise programs. These tenants, while having a "national" name are really regional or local for credit purposes. The credit behind the lease is only as strong as the franchisee (which could be very strong or marginal), unless the franchiser has guaranteed the lease.

Destination

Destination tenants do not rely on drive-by traffic or anchors to generate business. They derive business by selling specialized products or services and can include restaurants and theaters.

Some tenants that lenders don't necessarily care for are churches, local restaurants, dry cleaners, nightclubs or bars, pawnshops, as these type of tenants tend to have scattered lease structures. They typically don't keep really good financials, and it's hard to prove that they're actually profitable, especially for pawnshops and churches. Most of their business is typically "cash business". Their lease structures are not as favorable as other tenants, and not to mention, who wants to foreclose on a church? When those types of tenants are not in your property, you'd be in a better position to get the maximum leverage and favorable financing.

In this chapter, you learned:

1. *What a capitalization rate is and how it's used to value real estate.*
2. *The different types of lease structures available and how you can change your lease structure to obtain more favorable loan terms.*
3. *How lenders categorize tenants and lease terms, why they are important, and what tenants to stay away from.*

YOUR HOMEWORK:

Take a look at your leases and see what types of tenants you have in your building. Then see if you have a tenant that you may be able to replace with a more credit-worthy tenant. Calculate your cash flow and apply a cap rate. How does that affect your value? By replacing weaker tenants with stronger tenants, you will see how much more profitable your commercial real estate property can be.

CHAPTER TWO

What You Can Do to Achieve Maximum Cash Flow

Cash flow is what you receive after all of your expenses are paid. In commercial real estate, cash flow is expressed as either the Net Operating Income (NOI) of the property, the Cash Flow after Debt Service or Before Tax Cash Flow (BTCF) – if debt is included, or an After Tax Cash Flow (ATCF) which calculates the cash flow after the taxes are paid. In this chapter, we will focus on the Cash Flow After Debt Service or Before Tax Cash Flow (BTCF).

Achieving positive cash flow has to do with factors relating to the income the property produces and its annual expenses. In short, these are the only two ways to increase the cash flow of your asset: increasing the property's income and/or decreasing its expenses. Your annual debt service is also an expense, so you must consider this as well. You will usually see the debt service subtracted from the NOI to give you the BTCF.

In this chapter, we're going to look at what you can do to increase your cash flow, assuming you already own a property, while specifically focusing on increasing your property's income and decreasing your property's expenses. I will also briefly touch on how to increase your going in cash flow if you are looking to acquire another building.

What is the "Value Add" and How Do I Find It?

Value add is an enhancement in a property's value prior to offering the use of the property to its tenants. That is to say that you increase the income of the asset by creating value where it may not have been before. Before we get into the nitty-gritty of this, it's only prudent to go over how to calculate your annual cash flow. If you know this, great! You're in for a refresher.

POTENTIAL GROSS REVENUE (PGR)
   (-) General Vacancy & Collection Losses
   (+) Miscellaneous Income
EFFECTIVE GROSS REVENUE

OPERATING EXPENSES
   (-) Contract Services (Landscaping & Janitorial)
   (-) Repairs & Maintenance
   (-) Management Fee
   (-) Insurance
   (-) Real Estate Taxes
   (-) Replacement Reserves

NET OPERATING INCOME (NOI)
   (-) Annual Debt Service

BEFORE TAX CASH FLOW (BTCF)

The above illustrates how to find your before tax cash flow; Your Potential Gross Revenue minus (-) the Operating Expenses to get your NOI. From there, you will deduct your Annual Debt Service to calculate your BTCF. Make sense? We will go over each line item in the underwriting section of this book, but for now, let's discuss what it means to you if you increase your property's Effective Gross

Revenue.

The Effective Gross Revenue (EGR) is the Potential Gross Revenue of a property minus (-) the current vacancy and collection loss. The Value Add is located in the line items above the Effective Gross Revenue.

So the first question you have to ask yourself is "What will your tenants pay for"? For example, if you own a multifamily building, tenants tend to pay more for upgraded kitchens, bathrooms, floors, reserved parking, and access to laundry or washers and dryers. For the sake of space, I will use a real multifamily example of how one owner increased the EGR by focusing on the Value Add.

The owner purchased the multifamily property in 2014 from a well-known broker in Orlando, FL. The property's specifications are below:

- Purchase Price – $5,800,000
- 100% Occupied
- Cap Rate – 6.01%
- Lot Size – 0.31 +/- Acres
- Rentable Square Feet – 20,080
- Year built – 1989
- Units – 80
- Potential Gross Revenue - $584,480
- Effective Gross Revenue - $566,547
- Expenses - $217,971
- Net Operating Income - $348,576

We will discuss each line item in Chapter 8, but for now, let's get into how this owner increased income. From the above, you'd probably assume that the juice is squeezed out of this deal. Believe it or not, the owner felt the same way and was thinking about selling the property. After he and I sat down and talked about his goals, we were able to discover that there was still opportunity there. He renovated some of the bathrooms and kitchens, and updated washers and dryers in the units. He also increased his 'Miscellaneous Income' by maximizing his maintenance person who he was paying for anyway. Needless to say, instead of selling the property, he added over $100,000 in cash flow and $1,300,000 to the value of this asset! We will go into detail of how he accomplished this in a later chapter, but the basic idea here is creating the value add by implementing at the property what the tenants will pay for.

How to Reduce My Expenses to Increase My Cash Flow?

To reiterate, achieving a positive cash flow has to do with factors relating to the income the property produces and its annual expenses. Let's focus on reducing annual expenses including the debt service.

Operating expenses are typically broken down into two sections:

Fixed Expenses – expenses that are out of your control and will be the same amount regardless. An example would be taxes and insurance.

Variable Expenses – expenses that you can control and can be reduced or increased depending on how you manage your property like utilities and debt (they both have a fixed component, but there's some variability on them).

If you want to decrease your expenses, you want to focus on reducing the cost of variable expenses. As in the example above, the multifamily owner replaced his management company – from 6% of the effective rent ($33,992) to 4% of the effective rent ($22,661) and restructured the debt on the property. The debt on the property was 70% LTV, 3.85% interest rate, 5-year term, and a 20-year amortization. This equaled an annual debt service of $290,480. With the Net Operating Income of $348,000, the Before Tax Cash Flow is $58,096. I was able to help him increase his cash position by refinancing the property at 75% LTC, 4.25%, 10-year term, and a 30-year amortization with 2 years of interest only. This gave him a tax-free check for $290,000 at closing and a BTCF of $165,119 for the next two years – during the interest only period. Keep in mind, this is BEFORE the EGR was increased. The cash out proceeds would be used to increase the EGR.

Once this property was stabilized to its maximum potential the NOI skyrocketed to $450,000 per year, giving him a Before Tax Cash Flow to $255,686 for the following two years.

By doing a thorough look at his EGR and expenses, my client was able to increase his cash flow over $190,000 per year, bringing his cash on cash return to over 12.79%.

Why is Cash on Cash Return So Important?

The Equity Dividend Rate (EDR), or better known as the Cash on Cash Return, is the ratio between your annual debt service and the amount of equity you injected into the transaction. This return is taken into consideration the most during the acquisition of a property. Because this ratio is largely based on the debt service you have on your property, we will focus on how the lender will determine what debt to give you.

Lenders look at lending on a property in a couple different ways. One, like I mentioned before, who are your tenants? What are your lease structures? What's the condition of your property? Also, what is your financial position? Can you afford the payments if your building loses the majority of its tenants and couldn't cover the debt? A rule of thumb is that lenders want to see your net worth - your assets [which includes all the property you own] minus (-) your liabilities [which is all the debt that you are encumbered by] - equal to your loan amount and your post-closing liquidity [which is your liquid easily accessible cash] equal 10% of the loan amount or 9-12 months' P&I debt payments. This allows the lender to mitigate some of the risks associated with lending on a property that they will hold in their portfolio. The lender will also want to make sure your annual NOI will cover the debt service. To determine what the lender may be comfortable with, they use a metric called the Debt Service Coverage Ratio, or DSCR. This is calculated by dividing the annual Net Operating Income by the Annual Debt Service [NOI/ADS]. Many lenders in today's market need to see a debt coverage ratio of at least 1.25x on multifamily and 1.30x on other property types. This shows that the cash flow is healthy and if the property suffers a 25% - 30% decrease in income, it would still produce enough to pay the annual debt.

If you're in a position to refinance your property and you notice that the interest rates are at its lowest, you should definitely do that. So, first, take a look at where your interest rate position is today. Another thing to look at is, where is your amortization period? Are you sitting on a 20-year amortization? If so, you could benefit from a 25 or a 30-year amortization, which could allow you to improve your cash flow like in the example above.

Now, let's say you're looking to acquire an asset. We're going to use simple numbers to wrap our hands around this. Let's assume you are looking to acquire a property at a $1 million dollar acquisition price.

The lender may require at least $250,000 to be injected into the acquisition, which means that you'd receive 75% leverage on the transaction. Let me give you the basic specifications of this example:

30-Unit Multifamily
Loan amount – $750,000
Equity Requirement- $250,000
Rate – 4.25%
Amortization – 20 years
Annual Debt Service - $55,731
Net Operating Income - $70,000
Cap Rate – 7%
COC (EDR) – 5.71%

In the example above, your Cash on Cash Return is 5.71%. This means that on $250,000, you're making 5.71%. On the onset, this is a terrible return on your investment, especially as it relates to the cap rate, but let's see what most investors don't consider. As we discussed before, there's always more juice in a deal for you to squeeze profit out of. But let's assume you want to walk into this transaction with a higher cash on cash return. An immediate action you could take is increasing the amortization. Although this may result in a 10-15 basis point increase in your rate, it will still have a positive impact on your cash flow. Let's take a look at what happens when we increase your amortization and rate below:

30-Unit Multifamily
Loan amount – $750,000
Equity Requirement – $250,000
Rate – 4.35%
Amortization – 25 years
Annual Debt Service – $49,262

Net Operating Income - $70,000
Cap Rate – 7%
COC (EDR) – 8.30%

30-Unit Multifamily
Loan amount – $750,000
Equity Requirement– $250,000
Rate – 4.5%
Amortization – 30 years
Annual Debt Service – $55,731
Net Operating Income – $70,000
Cap Rate – 7%
COC (EDR)   9.76%

As you can see from the above, getting a longer amortization helps improve your cash on cash return. Most investors assume it's the rate on the money that is the driving force in a lower payment. Although this is the case to some extent, the father of all cash on cash issues is the amortization schedule. The reason this works is that as you stretch out the **amortization**, the **loan constant** decreases. If the loan constant is below the cap rate, you will achieve a higher return than the cap rate. This is called **positive leverage**. So, in using the examples above, you can compare the COC, or Equity Dividend Rate (EDR), Cap rate, and loan constant to understand this relationship:

	Cap Rate	Cash On Cash (EDR)	Loan Constant
Loan Option 1	7%	5.71%	7.43%
Loan Option 2	7%	8.30%	6.57%
Loan Option 3	7%	9.76%	6.08%

Some investors would prefer to keep the amortization lower in order to pay the property off sooner. Although having a longer amortization means that you will reduce principal at a slower rate, depending on how your loan is structured, you may be permitted to pay down your principal balance as much as you want without a penalty. In doing this, you can still achieve the cash flow you're looking for, while also paying down the mortgage on the property. Keep in mind, the leverage on this asset is what Robert Kiyosaki from Rich Dad, Poor Dad would call "good debt" because this debt is being used to leverage an asset that builds wealth and positive, passive income. That said, why pay it off?

Here's What You Now Know...

1. *How to calculate your before tax cash flow, debt service coverage ratio, and cash on cash return (equity dividend rate)*
2. *The father of all cash on cash issues is the amortization – not necessarily the rate*
3. *The two ways to increase your overall cash flow – increasing your property's income and decreasing your property's variable expenses*

YOUR HOMEWORK:

First, take a look at where your interest rate position is today. Also, where is your amortization schedule? Are you sitting on a 20-year amortization? Could you increase your return on equity by increasing your amortization even if it means increasing your interest rate? Check your line items and ensure that you're maximizing the profitability of your property. Can you reduce some of your expenses? Think of ways you could increase your EGR. Doing these things will put you well on your way to fully maximizing your property's cash flow.

CHAPTER THREE

What to do to Get the Best and Lowest Interest Rate Available?

A *common misconception is that the "best rate" is always the "lowest rate" in the market. This is not necessarily the case. Not only does it depend on the type of lender that you're working with, but it also depends on your goals and what you're looking to accomplish.*

For example, if you purchase a property that is not stabilized, it may be a great candidate for a bridge loan. A bridge loan is a short-term loan that will allow you to acquire a property, renovate the property, and refinance or sell the property at a higher value. These loans typically allow owners to leverage much higher than one would be able to with conventional financing, it's flexible and most often offers an interest-only term, it's based highly on the property's potential and your experience as an investor. Not to mention, these loans can close pretty quickly. The downside to bridge loans is that they can carry a rate about 3%-5% higher than conventional debt and lender fees are 2-3% of the loan amount. So let's look at an example.

Let's say you have a four-tenant retail property that you're considering acquiring that has a current NOI of $100,000 and is 50% occupied – which means two tenants occupy the property. The property is currently on the market for $900,000. You estimate that it will take about $100,000 to reface the property and take care of the landscape. Now, let's assume you have market data that suggests a local tenant and a national tenant are looking in the area to lease. You approach the potential tenants and ask if they would consider renting your vacant space, and they showed extreme interest. After the conversation with the potential national credit tenant, you get on the phone and call five other potential credit-worthy tenants just as you did with the first potential tenant. After you are confident in your research and find that there is truly an interest, you put the property under contract and approach a local bank for financing. The lender says that the property has potential but is only willing to lend 50% of the purchase price at a 20-year amortization. This means that you would need $450,000 equity into the purchase. Although your rate would be about 4.5%, you would be literally out $450,000[3]. Now, on the other hand, let's say you approached a bridge lender. The lender quoted you a loan with 75% of COST, or $750,000. This means that you will need $150,000 to get into the deal and $100,000 to fix up the property. Your rate would be about 8%. Which rate is the "best rate"? Let's see:

	Rate	Required Equity	Rehab Costs	Annual Payment	Savings
Conventional	4.50%	$ 450,000.00	$ 100,000.00	$ 34,163.00	
Bridge	8.00%	$ 150,000.00	$ 100,000.00	$ 35,656.00	
	Total	$ 350,000.00	0	(1,493)	$348,507.00

Now, it appears that the best rate in this case is actually the bridge rate. Why? Well, by paying an extra $1,493 a year, you save approximately $350,000 in required equity. Overall, your savings of $348,507 will make this rate a "better rate" and this is before we

---

[3] Please understand that this is an example. There are some commercial lenders that will lend with the new lease in mind.

discuss the potential after you lease up the other two units in the next two years.

What Are Interest Rates and How Are They Set?

Interest rates for investment properties are based on a spread over a certain index. An index is a financial indicator that rises and falls based on economic fluctuation[4]. The index that a lender uses may be the U.S. Treasury Bond rate, the constant maturity treasury rate, the Wall Street Journal prime rate, or the London Interbank Offered Rate, known as LIBOR for short.

The U.S. Treasury Bond rates are typically coterminous with the term of a loan. This means that if you visit your community bank for a commercial real estate loan, and they offer you a five-year term, they're more than likely going to price it over the five-year treasury rate. The spread – the difference between the index and the quoted interest rate – represents the lender's profit. It is measured in basis points (bps) and represents the lender's opinion of the how risky the investment is. Depending upon the property type, age, location, quality of income stream or leases, and your credit profile, spreads can range from 180 bps to 300+ bps.

In December of 2015, the Federal Reserve increased the federal funds rate, also called the overnight lending rate, by 25 basis points (0.25%). This was the first interest rate increase since the Great Recession. Increasing the federal funds rate, which is what banks charge each other to borrow funds from each other, immediately affected the WSJ prime rate. The prime rate is commonly used as a benchmark for short-term lending in the United States. It is set by

---

[4] *Mortgage Financing and Life Insurance Protection.* DOHRN INSURANCE TRAINING, INC., 2009, dohrnit.com/files/CE_MLIP_Text.pdf.

applying a 300 basis point spread over the highest target range of the federal funds rate. As of June 2019, the federal funds rate has a target range of 2.25% to 2.50%. Spreading that over 300 basis points, you're looking at a prime rate today of 5.50%. Keep in mind, the prime rate before the hike in 2015 was 3.25%. Although, we are currently in a rising interest rate environment, if you're looking to refinance or acquire new property, now's the time to do it while rates are still fairly low.

Although indexes may fluctuate at times, spreads can also rise or fall depending on perceived risk in a market or at a specific lending institution. For example, in 2016, a community bank in Tampa, FL was known to be very aggressive on small multi-tenant retail buildings under $2.5 million with a spread of 205 over the 5 year treasury rate. By the end of 2016, they had overextended funds to retail and were practically "tapped out". Not only was their retail bucket full, but also the incurred bad debt from lazy underwriting on these property types. In 2017, the community bank decided internally to increase their spread from 205 to 255 – which was closer to market rate. Almost overnight, interest rates for neighborhood strip centers increased by .50% due to the bank's perception that neighborhood strip centers carried increased risk, even though the Fed Funds Rate, the indexes, spreads, and interest rates for other types of loans remained unchanged. Keep in mind that money is a commodity. Like the price of oil, interest rates and terms can change overnight with market news.

What Are "Safe Rates" and Why Do Lenders Use Them?

Many of my clients come to me from a referral. The referral is usually a commercial real estate broker or capital markets advisor who is looking to help their client secure financing to either acquire a property that the broker has listed or refinance a current property.

Usually, I get an email like the following:

Charles,

I have a buyer who is putting on offer on the attached property in NJ tonight. They will most likely buy it with cash and then put financing on it after they close. The buyer has hundreds of millions of dollars and would like to know what kind of rates and term he would be able to get under the following scenarios:

Non-Recourse	Recourse
10 year term	10 year term
15+ year term	15+ year term

Would it be possible for you to get me some quick quotes by 4pm today?

Thanks!

Excuse the misspelling but that's the exact email I received from a commercial broker a few weeks back. The problem with this email is that it provides little to no information on the borrower, no information on their overall goals, which could affect their amortization schedule, nothing on what's important to the borrower, and literally wants a "soft quote" in a few hours. Unlike a preliminary quote or term sheet, a soft quote carries a ton of assumptions. I never recommend soft quotes, as they are a poor reflection on what lenders are able to do specifically for a borrower. As you can imagine, my answer was "Give me your client's number so that I may speak with them about their options".

In a low interest rate or rising interest rate market like we're in today, please be very cautious about obtaining a soft quote from any lender. Never call a bank or capital provider and ask "Hey, what rate can you offer me on the property down the street?" Obviously, the capital provider knows nothing about you and can only give general terms of what their balance sheets will allow. Unfortunately, your rates could be much higher and your terms much worse than what's quoted.

You recall in the previous chapter that lenders apply a Debt Service Coverage Ratio (DSCR) to a property's Net Operating Income to determine the amount of cash flow available for debt service. You can easily determine what your max allowable debt will be by using the calculator on your cell phone to solve for the loan amount that will be achievable; i.e, NOI/DSCR. Commercial real estate brokers are notorious for adding incorrect debt options to their sales packages by describing how a property can be purchased with a down payment of "X," a loan amount of "Y," and a cash on cash return of "Z." But then when you apply for a loan in a low interest or rising interest rate market, it's discovered that a considerably lower loan amount is available and a considerably higher down payment is required. What went wrong?

Nothing. The lender (as they all do) simply "stressed" the NOI with a "safe rate." A safe rate is an arbitrary interest rate applied by lenders when underwriting DSCRs. It is most commonly used in a rising interest rate market to protect the lender against a spike in interest rates. The safe rate is whatever each lender chooses it to be at the time the lender chooses to apply it. It can change without notice, it's not published, and cannot be predicted.

For example, at a debt coverage of 1.30, a loan with an interest rate of 4.5% and a quoted LTV of 75% could have a debt coverage of 1.03 if the interest is stressed to a 6.0% rate. Thus, the lender might choose to underwrite the loan at a "safe rate" of 6.0%. Looking at the math, applying a 1.30 DSCR to an NOI of $240,000 at a starting rate of 4.5% amortized over 25 years suggests that a loan of $2,767,851 is attainable. However, when the lender stresses the rate to 6.0%, only $2,387,798 is attainable – nearly 15% less! That said, when you gather quotes, make sure to ask your lender how they are stressing *their loans during underwriting.*

Here's What You Now Know...

1. *What is an interest rate and how it is set.*
2. *What is a stress rate and why you should NEVER settle for a soft quote when seriously considering a loan purchase or refinance.*
3. *That money is a commodity. Like the price of oil, interest rates and terms can change overnight with market news.*

YOUR HOMEWORK...

Take a look at your loan docs. What's your interest rate? Can you tell how it was priced and what index was used? What bank did you get your loan from? Ask the lender how they are currently stressing their rates. The next time you inquire about a loan, make sure to stress your rates like this bank in order to prevent a re-trade.

Section II

How to Get Your Deal Financed With Max Cash Flow and the Lowest Rate Guaranteed! How Do You Find the Best Lender For Your Situation?

In the first section, we discussed ways to maximize your property, in a very general way. In the second section, we're going to discuss HOW to achieve the best rates in the market, the highest cash flow, and an increase in your property's value. The following chapters may appear daunting, but don't fear. My goal is to help you become competent at this, allowing you to easily increase the value of your asset and get the best debt available in today's market.

In the coming chapters, we will be discussing the following:

- ***How to Underwrite Your Property Like a Lender for Maximum Value***
    - *This will help you manage your risk as well as work with lenders in the marketplace.*
- ***How to Maximize Your Cash Flow***
    - *Understanding how to implement cash flow enhancing tools to SKYROCKET your cash flow.*
- ***How to Get the Best Rates Available in Today's Market?***
    - *Finally you can CUT YOUR current INTEREST*

>   RATE or refinance to obtain a lower interest rate today!

Before we get into the "How" section of the book, let's discuss lenders for a moment. This is important because each "type" of lender underwrites differently. Knowing which buttons to push will give you a leg up in your discussions with them. There are four classes of lenders that I will discuss with you.

- Conduit lenders, including Fannie Mae and Freddie Mac lenders.
    - They're arbitrageurs that use a credit line to borrow money from, and they borrow that money from Wall Street to make real estate loans at an interest rate of x, as an example. They then package those loans together and sell them in commercial mortgage backed securities, sell them in a package to investors in the secondary market at a certain yield. Then they make the spread between x and y, so rate x and yield y. These lenders tend to be a bit more risky. They also provide favorable loan structures, and have great terms that are focused on longer amortizations, longer terms, and higher leverage.

- A Bank or Credit Union.
    - Now, the banks and credit unions are the most common to deal with when financing commercial assets. They both achieve their lending power by using money from deposit relationships that they develop over the years. Banks and credit unions make their profit also on spread. They typically use either a

yield on the shorter end of the yield curve, or they tie it to the Wall Street Journal prime rate.

- Life Insurance Companies.
    - Insurance companies, they use a portion of their insurance policy profits to make loans as a part of a diversified investment strategy. They hold some of the loans on their balance sheet, the ones that have the least amount of risk, and they sell the loans on the secondary market that has the most risk tied to it. They also make their profit on the interest rate spread, and they usually spread over the treasury or swaps, whatever is less. Insurance that is typically only available for class A, class B properties, and primary and secondary mortgages. The tertiary product is not going to be a good fit for an insurance company.
- Private equity, which also includes bridge debt and hard money debt, "soft" money debt.
    - Although these loans tend to have higher interest rates, starting somewhere around 6% and could be as high as 14%, they tend to offer the most flexibility, so if you have a property that's 50% occupied, you want to get into the property, acquire the property, fix the property, and then dispose of the property. A bridge loan would offer you quick access to funding within a two/three-week turnaround, with no prepayment liability, and you could be in and out of that transaction within six months, and at times, it's also the best strategy to take when looking for debt financing.

Now that you understand the different types of commercial real estate lenders in the marketplace, let's forge ahead and discuss the "How" to cut your rate, maximize your property's value, and secrets that property owners do not know.

CHAPTER FOUR

Underwriting the Lender Way for Maximum Profitability

When reviewing your property for financing or for sale, it is important to have a good understanding of the four essential components of a deal and ALWAYS complete a Performance Level Assessment (PLA). A PLA allows you to understand the dynamics of how the deal can be underwritten to accomplish various objectives. In this chapter, we will go over the following:

- *The Real Estate*
- *The Market*
- *Underwriting the Numbers*
- *Sponsor - Owner/Developer - Track Record, Financial Strength*

Having the above data is important because the lender's underwriter will examine your income tax returns (especially if you're looking at obtaining financing through a bank), credit reports, property appraisal and inspection reports, conduct his/her own analysis of the property's income and expenses for the prior 24 to 36 months, and may make an exterior inspection of the property and the surrounding neighborhood. Based upon this final analysis, the underwriter is authorized to re-underwrite the appraiser's NOI and value conclusions and make recommendations to the loan committee. If you have the above items in order, you can make recommendations that can result in modifications to the approved LTV, rate, and loan terms.

What Do I Need to Understand About the Real Estate?

Many factors relating to understanding your real estate you already know like the back of your hand: the property address, the property type, the number of buildings or units, and how to access the property. But when you're considering a loan to acquire or refinance a property, the lender will also need to know what type of construction the building is, what shape the roof is in or is there any other deferred maintenance, the gross and net rentable sf., the bay depths/widths if you have an industrial building, any flood zone considerations, and what was located at and surrounding the property prior to its current use. In addition to this, a property zoning report may also be required which will include the current zoning of the property, the parking ration, and allowed uses of the property.

What Do I Need to Understand About the Market?

Understanding the market takes a lot of time and research, and can be a useful hobby to pick up. Appraisers spend a lot of time deciphering the market, doing rent surveys, and studying sales. This is why lenders tend to lean on their expertise when determining the value of an asset. The lender will assign an appraiser to conduct an opinion of value of the property. Appraisers are technical writers who must prove their conclusions with data from the market and mathematical formulae. The appraiser will inspect and tape measure the square footage of the property's interior and exterior; review any leases or rental agreements; review your income and expense statements for the previous 36 months; conduct independent rent and sales surveys (appraisers are required to contact one of the principals in all comparable sales transactions to confirm income, price and terms data, and to include the contact's name and phone number in the appraisal report); and determine a realistic NOI. The appraisal is then reviewed by another appraiser at the financing institution looking for improper appraisal technique or illogic in the initial appraiser's conclusions. You should take a look at the questions below, and ask yourself, do I know the answers? If not, you have some homework to do.

- *Where the real estate is positioned in relation to the market competition and evaluate the location. i.e., on a frontage road, hedge, shrubbery, fences or trees obstructing visibility, awkwardly developed, signage is not visible, etc.*
- *Is the neighborhood stable, declining, or improving?*
- *How far is the property to freeways, major streets, and related uses?*
- *Does this property look like it belongs in this location at this time?*
- *What is the market vacancy?*
- *If you own a retail building, what is the average daily traffic count (ADT) near your property?*
- *If you have acquired a value-added asset that has multiple vacancies, what is the absorption rate in the market?*

If you find that you do not know one or more of the answers to the questions above, an easy way to find out is to create and maintain relationships with national real estate firms that compile absorption statistics by market or submarket and talk with an appraiser who knows the market.

How Do I Underwrite the Numbers Like a Lender?

In order to underwrite your property like the lenders who will be lending you money, you have to know how they will view your income. To recap what I discussed in Chapter Two, below is how to calculate your Before Tax Cash Flow:

POTENTIAL GROSS REVENUE (PGR)
   (-) General Vacancy & Collection Losses
   (+) Miscellaneous Income
EFFECTIVE GROSS REVENUE

OPERATING EXPENSES
   (-) Contract Services (Landscaping & Janitorial)
   (-) Repairs & Maintenance
   (-) Management Fee
   (-) Insurance
   (-) Real Estate Taxes
   (-) Replacement Reserves

NET OPERATING INCOME (NOI)
   (-) Annual Debt Service

BEFORE TAX CASH FLOW (BTCF)

How Do Most Lenders View Income and Expenses?

The way you would potentially underwrite a property's income and expenses to sell your property often differs from the way a lender will underwrite the same property for lending purposes. If you are aware of these differences, you will be better prepared to prevent misunderstandings and have a more realistic view of what to expect when refinancing your current property or financing your next commercial investment property.

Following are the line items that most often lead to unrealistic expectations and disappointment when obtaining a loan.

Base Rent

More often than not, investors tend to buy "End of Year One" Net Operating Income; which is, the NOI that the buyer will collect after the first 12 months of ownership, including scheduled rent increases. However, the current lending market will only recognize rent increases that are scheduled to occur within three to six months after the loan closing, except where the tenant has strong national or regional credit. On a case-by-case basis, increases to high quality income streams may be recognized out to 12 months.

Percentage Rent in Retail Properties

If you receive any percentage rent, you may be counting the entire amount of percentage income. However, percentage rent is not a given. In an economy on the downswing, overage income that was at one time an expected event may be whittled down to nothing. Lenders will look for the history, quality, and probability of continuance of the percentage rent and may give a deep (50% or more) discount to this income.

"Miscellaneous" Income

If the income can't be counted on, it won't be recognized. Examples would be late fees, returned check fees, key fees, and interest income on deposits. If you have scheduled miscellaneous income that can be proved, then this will be counted towards your NOI.

Vacancy

According to appraisers and underwriters, 5% vacancy is 100%

occupied. Lenders may apply (i) the greater of market vacancy or 5%; (ii) the property's occupancy history; (iii) the property's current vacancy; or (iv) any other number they choose in their underwriting, in spite of any opinions from the seller, the buyer, the broker, and the appraiser to the contrary.

Off-Site Management

This expense must always be included. Lenders work under the assumption that they will have to undertake foreclosure of the property at some future date and will have to hire third-party management until disposition of the property. Fees typically range from 4% to 8% of all monies collected, including expense reimbursements.

Replacement Reserves

Many lenders will require reserves to be included above line when calculating the NOI. The replacement reserve account is monies put aside for replacing major items on the property, such as roofs, appliances, parking lots, and similar capital improvements. Depending upon the region in which the property is located, lenders' underwriters are currently applying $250 – $350 per unit for apartments, and $0.15 – $0.25 per square foot for commercial properties. As these monies are held in longer term accounts, they generally earn interest.

Tenant Improvements and Leasing Commissions Reserve (Office and Retail)

Reserve amounts are a "below the line" expense that you will probably not include in your NOI underwriting for marketing purposes. Lenders, however, may add this expense "above the line" in their underwriting if the property has a significant amount of short-term leases or if there is a large tenant turnover in the property's local market[5]. T.I. and leasing commission reserves are based upon the number of times each lease will roll (or expire), applied against historical lease commissions and tenant improvement costs. For purposes of underwriting the NOI, most lenders require reserves of approximately $0.60 to $1.00 per square foot for leasing commissions and tenant improvements. If you can demonstrate to the lender (usually by way of a rent survey) that standard lease negotiations in the market cause tenants to conduct their own interior improvements, the lender may reduce this amount.

So what do you do with this information?

If your property has been stabilized for at least two years, create a side-by-side comparison or Property Level Analysis over the last two years. Adjacent to that, do an appraisal estimate using the income and expenses you feel the appraiser will use – using the above as a guide. Keep in mind, you want to make sure your Potential Gross Revenue is showing the maximum amount you could be receiving if 100% of the building is leased up with the current rental agreements in place. The rental rates would need to be backed up by some sort of rent comparable.

Now, if your property is not stabilized – meaning that there are higher than market vacancies – how much of stretch, if any, are the proposed rents? What is really market rent for the property? What is the market trend in recent years? Now look at the expenses and inflate them 3% per year for an estimate of what they will be when the property is at stabilized occupancy.

---

[5] "Above the line" or "Below the line" refers to whether the expense is calculated to get the NOI or if it's listed after calculating the NOI

Understanding the Borrower

When approaching a lender to refinance your property, remember, they're in it for the long haul; they want to get to know you, as they are relationship based. Unfortunately, 95% of the time borrowers approach the wrong person when looking for a commercial real estate loan and may not understand this right away. For example, at a bank, you have business development officers, market leaders, commercial business bankers, or commercial lenders who will have to either contact someone else to work with you or pitch your property to their credit committee.

The credit committee is the investment panel who makes the decision whether or not to lend on your property. This committee is usually made up of the Chief Credit Officer, Chief Investment Officer, Chief Business Services Officer, and other executives of the financial institution. Part of the lender's presentation to the credit committee is describing who the sponsor or borrower is and their experience.

The committee will want to see what your personal financial picture consists of. You will be asked to fill in a personal financial statement which will show your current net worth, liquidity, your current real estate holdings, current debt of those holdings, your current cash flow situation, and details on your outside income. For the lender to be comfortable, your net worth and liquidity is extremely important when reviewing debt options. To reiterate, your liquidity is the cash/assets you can liquidate, and your net worth is your assets minus your current liabilities. In reviewing your real estate portfolio, the lender will compare your portfolio's value to your current debt. A debt position of 50% or below is preferred, as it will have an effect on your total net worth.

When reviewing your commercial real estate investment experience, some lenders may require references from banks who have provided financing for you. This is not usually a requirement, but having it available will help the lender feel a little more comfortable in working with you.

Having these documents is really the first step. Other information and documentation that will be valuable for the lender to have is:

- *Prepared business P&L statements*
- *Income trends on your tax returns over the last three years*
- *Your business ownership structure*
- *Do you have any default history or bankruptcy issues that the lenders will find out during their due diligence?*
- *Do you have any second loans? This debt will have to be removed.*
- *Are there other partnership loans outstanding?*
- *Is your net worth and liquidity sufficient for a loan this size? Remember, as a rule of thumb, your net worth should be at least equal to the loan amount and you should have at least 10% of the liquidity in savings (after acquisition or before refinance).*
- *Are there any partnership problems?*

If you keep these in mind, you will be in good shape when providing your personal information to a lender for financing purposes.

You Mentioned Forms of Ownership. Can You Explain?[6]

Very briefly, there are a few types of ownership structures that you should understand so that you may effectively communicate your structure.

---

[6] This section is referenced from "Common Forms of Property Ownership." *FreeAdvice.com*, 1995, real-estate-law.freeadvice.com/real-estate-law/real-estate-law/property_ownership_forms.htm.

- *Individual: Property is owned entirely by one person. Words in the deed such as "John, a single man" establish title as individual ownership;.*
- *Partnership: Property is owned by two or more people and is equally split.*
- *TIC: Property is owned by two or more people but proportionate interests aren't the same.*
- *LLC: A limited liability company is the U.S.-specific form of a private limited company. It is a business structure that combines the pass-through taxation of a partnership or sole proprietorship with the limited liability of a corporation.*
- *Corporation: A company or group of people authorized to act as a single entity (legally a person) and recognized as such in law.*

Here's What You Now Know...

1. *How to create a PLA – property level assessment and what are the four essential components of a deal that lenders need to know before making a decision to lend on your property*
2. *How to underwrite in a lender favorable way so that you can achieve the best terms without surprises during the loan process*
3. *How to underwrite yourself as a borrower and now know what lenders look for*

YOUR HOMEWORK:

Take a look at your financials and see if you can complete a basic PLA using the tools discussed in this chapter. Do your property level financials include any miscellaneous income? Can you prove this income? In looking at the four components of a deal - What are some ways you could argue that your property could be worth more today than it was when you purchased it? What has changed?

CHAPTER FIVE

Three Questions You Never Ask That Can Add Over $1,000,000 in Current Value to Your Property

What I'm about to tell you is a little known secret that many investors would not consider – and that's <u>beefing up your NOI by increasing the miscellaneous income</u>. We're going to piggy-back on an earlier chapter on how to increase your cash flow by focusing on what your tenant will pay for. Let's revisit this line item below.

As you learned in the previous chapter, miscellaneous income is usually a line item used to count laundry room income, parking income, and rental income for community center use. What most people don't realize is that the miscellaneous income line item holds a tremendous amount of value that could be taken advantage of in commercial real estate. I'm going to give you some ideas to increase this number and potentially add thousands to your bottom line.

The first thing you want to do is determine again, What Will Your Tenants Pay For? Using the example in Chapter Two, the multifamily owner increased his income over $100,000 a year by manipulating this line item and his overall income. When I met with the owner [let's call him Jim] and reviewed his situation, I noticed that he was paying for an on-site maintenance person. This maintenance person was paid $9 per hour for 40 hours per week and was also given an apartment to live in for free. This was costing Jim about $18,720 in wages and $7,300 in free rent for a total of $26,020. Now, it wasn't like Jim used the maintenance man the entire 40 hours every workweek. In other words, the maintenance man was on call so that if there were any issues, he would go out and fix the necessary problems. Jim had a choice, get rid of the maintenance man and hire a part-time maintenance person to cut his current maintenance expenses 40% or use the maintenance person to increase the miscellaneous income. So we weighed both options, and Jim decided to explore using the maintenance man for more than what he was paying him for. These are the three questions I asked Jim that helped him add over $1M in value to his property.

1. What assets do you have that are being underutilized?

The first thing I asked Jim was what assets he owned that he wasn't using to its fullest potential. Well, we know that the maintenance man wasn't being used for the full 40 hours, so that's one. I also noticed that a truck was parked near the management office and it seemed to sit there most of the day. I came to find out that the truck belonged to the maintenance man.

2. How can you utilize the assets?

So here we have a person and a truck – can we do anything with that? Well, I noticed that the multifamily asset was about 8 miles away from a large university. We decided to use the truck on the weekends to help students move from one dorm to another- while also marketing the apartment units as VIP Tenant Suites. So the maintenance person put out flyers along with a sign on the road *stating that they were local movers with the best rates on the market – One Man and a Truck.*

In addition to this, the owner decided to include a VIP tenant package which included reserved parking in the newly reserved covered parking area and trash pickup two days per week. This was an additional service that tenants paid $150 extra per month for. Tenants could also pay separately for each service - $100 for the carport and $50 for the trash pickup.

3. *If you implement the above, what will be the result?*

Because Jim was able to utilize assets that he already had, he was able to use the maintenance person as a part-time mover and use an already accessible truck to do the moving. The maintenance man was given a gas stipend of $200 per month. He averaged about $2000 per month or $24,000 per year doing this.

Jim spent roughly $100,000 to build the covered carport. With 40 tenants paying for the reserved parking and 70 tenants paying for the trash pickup, the owner created an additional $80,000 per year.

The total miscellaneous income that the owner created was over $100,000, but the value of the property was still annualized at a 6% capitalization rate. This made the value increase over $1.7 million. Keep in mind – this took about two full years of cash flow to prove this property could achieve this value. Let me repeat that last bit of information in case you missed it; you will need to show two years' stabilized cash flow in order to refinance or sell at this value. This is the case because many owners beef up the cash flow to prepare for a sale or refinance. Lenders and buyers are aware of this and will not count the cash flow as true income.

There are other ways to increase cash flow that are more permanent.

One way is to create a VIP concept at your multifamily location where only 50% of the rooms are completely rehabbed – stainless steel, granite counters, brand new washer/dryers, etc. Now, the reason you'd want to only rehab half of the rooms is because you create a "VIP" feel to your property. You then charge a premium to anyone who wants to live in the VIP units. Let's assume it costs you $5,000 to renovate each unit because you receive a super cheap rehab package at a wholesale price. If you have 50 units in total, assume you rehab 25 of those units, which will cost you $125,000. Assuming the average rent is $1000 per month or roughly $555,000 gross income per year, you may potentially charge $1800 per month for the VIP units. Doing so, your total gross income will increase to over $840,000 per year. If all else remains equal, you will create an additional $285,000 per year to your bottom line.

Now, before you decide to do this, you should reach out to a professional to provide you with comparable market data to provide insight into what can be done for your property type. If possible, you should consider adding value to your property by refinancing, pulling cash out, and performing the renovations necessary to increase your value.

Here's What You Now Know...

1. *Ways to think about increasing your miscellaneous income, by thinking outside of the box*
2. *Miscellaneous income is the least utilized line item on the operating statement*
3. *How adding a VIP program at your property can add thousands to your bottom line and millions to your value*

YOUR HOMEWORK...

Ask yourself, "What will my tenants pay for?" Then ask yourself the three questions posed above. Look for any expenses or product that you may have access to that is being underutilized. Can your manager work part-time to bring income to the property? Finding out the small things that can be done will open your income pool up dramatically.

CHAPTER SIX

How to Negotiate Max Leverage While Also Achieving a Positive Cash-on-Cash Return

*N**egotiating the highest proceeds has much to do with your goals and how you manage your property's finances. If you're looking for maximum proceeds, especially if you're refinancing a property using conventional financing, you'll want to make sure that your tax returns and profit and loss statement reflect solid income. Investors tend to diminish their earnings by increasing expenses or other line items on their tax return in order to reduce their tax liability. Unfortunately, while doing this, investors also lessen their chances of refinancing at maximum levels, even when the P&L statements are showing adequate income. Because conventional lenders weigh the property's ability to cash flow heavily on what's reported on the tax returns, let's go over the income and expense statement taken directly from a sample tax return – specifically, Form 8825. Take a look at the below example of Form 8825 which shows an income and expense analysis on the property.*

Form **8825** (Rev. December 2010) Department of the Treasury Internal Revenue Service	Rental Real Estate Income and Expenses of a Partnership or an S Corporation ▶ See instructions on back. ▶ Attach to Form 1065, Form 1065-B, or Form 1120S.		OMB No. 1545-1186
Name			Employer identification number

1	Show the type and address of each property. For each rental real estate property listed, report the number of days rented at fair rental value and days with personal use. See instructions. See page 2 to list additional properties.			
	Physical address of each property—street, city, state, ZIP code	Type—Enter code 1-8; see page 2 for list	Fair Rental Days	Personal Use Days
A				

If you happen to compare the line items above and below to your Form 8825, you will notice that your property will be listed in the column labeled "A". Most investment properties have 365 Fair Rental Days and no personal use days annually. Below is a breakdown of how the line items are analyzed:

		A
Rental Real Estate Income		
Gross rents	2	184,490.
Rental Real Estate Expenses		
Advertising	3	1,656.
Auto and travel	4	1,217.
Cleaning and maintenance	5	2,760.
Commissions	6	525.
Insurance	7	6,600.
Legal and other professional fees	8	1,607.
Interest	9	55,851.
Repairs	10	17,196.
Taxes	11	36,535.
Utilities	12	8,911.
Wages and salaries	13	
Depreciation (see instructions)	14	33,332.
Other (list) ▶ SEE ATTACHED		21,211.
	15	
Total expenses for each property. Add lines 3 through 15	16	187,401.
Income or (Loss) from each property. Subtract line 16 from line 2	17	(2,911.)

Above, you will notice some similarities in the income and expense analysis on Form 8825 and the operating statement in the first section of the book. Your gross rents will be compared to what you're reporting on your rent roll, and commissions, interest, and depreciation will be removed from the above first. This is done in order to provide a positive cash flow scenario for the lender to analyze. In the above example, commission, interest, and depreciation equals $89,708; this will be added back to the net income. Most lenders will stop right there. From here, it will be your responsibility to discuss what repairs you've done to your property in the reported year of the tax return.

The "repairs" line item can be adjusted downward or can be completely removed if the repairs can be justified and categorized as capital expenditures. Capital expenditures, or CAPEX for short, can be removed if you can provide insight into the item that was repaired and provide proof that it was a onetime expense. For example, if you replaced the roof or added new carpet to all of your multifamily units, you would show this as a capital expenditure and add this back to your cash flow. This would provide an extra $17,196 to your NOI. Does this make a difference? Let's see below:

We're going to assume that this specific lender has a minimum Debt Service Coverage Ratio (DSCR) of 1.25x and is charging a 4% rate – underwritten at a 5% stress rate and a 20-year amortization. If the repairs are not explained and removed, the maximum loan amount that this borrower can achieve is $906,202. Now, in using the same exact parameters above, including the repair costs into the cash flow, the borrower's maximum loan amount is $1,079,911. Almost $175,000 more!

If your NOI is lower than where it needs to be, your value and loan will also be affected. In order to achieve maximum leverage, you want to make sure that your values are at its maximum, and to do that, you need to make sure that your expenses are showing accurately.

In our above example, let's assume the borrower had an $800,000 outstanding loan that will be paid off at closing. Looking at the numbers, the borrower could potentially cash out over $250,000 from this transaction. Now, although this money is technically yours, most lenders will not agree to give you cash out IF you don't have a plan for the funds. They may either require the remaining funds to be "controlled" in a lender managed reserve account, allowing the lender to monitor what you do with the funds, or they will only allow you to refinance enough to pay off your existing loan.

The key here is when you advise the lender that you're going to refinance the property and you're looking to pull cash out, also tell them that you're going to put $100,000 of your $250,000 back into the property and $150,000 into a new acquisition. You always want to say that you plan to put cash back into the property because the lender is also looking at that property as a major investment for them. The lenders want to know that you're committed to that property, and that you're going to maintain it with a portion of the equity. Now, whether you fix up the property or not, it's up to you, but make sure you tell them that you will.

My Bank Will Give Me the Cash-Out I'm Looking For, Right?

Most borrowers assume that their bank will provide the best loan option for them when considering a refinance. That may be the case, depending on how secure your deposit relationship is. If you recall in our previous discussion about lender types, banks and credit unions will lend the money that they have in deposits in order to generate a profit on the funds they're holding in their bank. If there's little bank deposits, then no matter how much your bank likes you, they won't be able to provide you with the best terms in the market. This includes lower than market rates and the highest possible leverage.

But let's assume that you work with a lender that you do a lot of business with. Your deposits are strong, and your relationship is stellar. What could go wrong? Eventually, what's going to happen is your relationship with that lender is going to be overextended. You see, every community lender has a cap or loan limit on how much any one client can borrow. Being overextended means that you have hit that cap or you're very close to it.

Years ago, as a capital markets advisor, I was introduced to a borrower who primarily developed quick service restaurants in the Tampa Bay area. He wanted to venture out and purchase his second multi-tenant retail building in Orlando, Florida. To no surprise, he reached out to the community bank where he did most of his business to inquire about securing a loan. His lender was very excited about it, and of course he wanted to lend on the property. The project was $4.5 million and he was looking to obtain 75% LTV or about $3.375 million. The borrower moved forward with his bank past his due diligence period and onward towards closing. Unfortunately, two weeks before closing, the lender informed the borrower that they could not lend what they had promised because the borrower was overextended.

When I got word from this borrower's broker, it was almost too late. As I was speaking with the borrower, he frantically expressed needing a quick solution, as his $200,000 earnest money deposit had already become nonrefundable. I was able to locate, in the nick of time, a new community lender that would provide the borrower the debt to acquire this new transaction by creating a new deposit relationship with this bank. This new lender requested that the borrower transferred his current deposits from his home bank to this *new community bank.*

Does this also apply to refinancing multifamily properties?

Depending on how you're looking to fund your refinance, multifamily has some of the best options in the market. As a multifamily loan advisor, I can tell you that higher leverage, longer terms, and lower rates make these loan options almost as good as owner occupied loans. Most conventional lenders have stopped allowing investors to cash out of their properties without scrutinized underwriting and very conservative terms. Without cash out, commercial banks and credit unions have limited leverage to 75% and amortizations to 20-25 years. For some, the benefit of these loans would be in the nonexistence of a prepayment penalty or a limited prepayment penalty that can be estimated upon acquisition. For others, the commercial bank is all they know. But there is another option to consider.

GSE's have been a major force in the multifamily lending industry since the Great Recession. Specifically, the Federal Home Loan Mortgage Corporation (FHLMC) or Freddie Mac and the Federal National Mortgage Association (FNMA) or Fannie Mae have provided loans for small private multifamily investors through their Small Balance Loan (SBL) or Small Mortgage Loan (SML) programs. These loans range from $1 million to $7.5 million and $1 million to $6 million, respectively. Some of the benefits of these loans are as follows:

- *Flexible loan terms – the ability to have a 5,7,or 10 year fixed rate loan.*
- *Very competitive rates – because the rate is not tied to WSJ Prime like that of the lenders, the rate is tied to the US*

treasury which can provide lower than market interest rates

- *Interest Only periods – In a previous chapter, we discussed how one multifamily investor was able to increase his cash-flow by incorporating an interest only period on his refinanced loan. This loan was through Freddie Mac's SBL program.*
- *Benefits for having affordable housing tenants – having section 8 tenants or homeless veteran tenants is seen as a negative when financing such property with a commercial bank or credit union. Freddie's SBL program provides a 20-40 bps decrease in interest rate for qualifying properties*
- *Fannie Mae offers supplemental loans – if there is a property that is acquired that has a Fannie Mae loan that was assumed, Fannie Mae will offer the borrower a second loan up to 80% total leverage on qualifying properties*
- *Fannie Mae offers self-liquidating loans*
- *30 year amortizations – which is key to increasing your property's cash flow*
- *Tax Returns ARE NOT required – Freddie and Fannie understand that tax returns aren't usually a good determination of how a property is performing due to the borrower wanting to reduce their tax liabilities. Because of this, an accurate rent roll and P&L statement will be enough.*
- *Cash Out is still a "thing" – You are able to achieve as much cash out that the property can handle. You would need to advise the lender why you are requesting the cash out and what you plan to do with it. This can be as simple as a few items on a word document.*

If you have a multifamily asset that you're considering to refinance and pull cash out, reach out to me and let's discuss how a GSE loan from Fannie Mae or Freddie Mac will work for you.

Here's What You Now Know...

1. *When you're putting together your property level analysis, make sure the numbers on your P&L statements are very close, if not exact, to the numbers on your Form 8825. The lenders will weigh your tax returns more heavily than your P&Ls.*
2. *Keeping track of your CAPEX can help increase your loan request tremendously. Having clean and well-organized records is very important when proving that a capital expenditure is not an ongoing expense.*
3. *Developing new deposit relationships can help increase your lending options when applying for a loan.*
4. *The benefits of a Freddie Mac and Fannie Mae loan and how going this route can be the best loan option for your multifamily asset.*

YOUR HOMEWORK...

Pull out your tax returns and review your Form 8825. Is the form putting your property in its best light? Take a look at your repairs line item. Can you categorize some of these repairs as CAPEX? Analyze your lender relationships. Who's your go-to lender? What's your deposit status with that lender? Can you establish a better relationship elsewhere? Community banks and credit unions are better for relationships. Make sure one of your relationships include either one of the two. Do you have a multifamily asset? Reach out to me and let's talk about how a Freddie Mac or Fannie Mae loan might be beneficial to you.

CHAPTER SEVEN

How to Use an Owner Occupied Trick to Get You Higher Leverage and the Lowest Possible Rate When Acquiring Your Next Property

So far we have been discussing investment property, but let's visit the idea of using a little know secret to obtain maximum leverage and the lowest interest rate in the marketplace. You will do this by applying for an owner occupied loan.

If you own a business, right now is probably the best time to finance an owner occupied property. Most owner occupied commercial assets are single or multi-tenant office, industrial, hospitality, retail, health care, and special purpose where the owner occupies or manages the real estate. Owners who are operating out of these asset types are able to obtain the lowest rates on the market and the longest term.

For example, one of my clients received a self-amortizing loan that was fixed for 20 years with a 20-year amortization at a staggering 4.60% rate. As a comparison, this rate is pretty close to a 5-year fixed rate term on an investment property. The borrower also was able to obtain an 80% loan to value where if the same property was acquired for an investment, the investor would only be able to achieve 70-75% max loan to value.

Owner occupied lending is based on the cash flow of the business to service the debt. Therefore, instead of reviewing leases, a bank reviews the health of the business through financial analysis. Now, in order to qualify for one of these loans, you must own a business and occupy at least 51% of the real estate.

So what's the secret here? How can you use this to create a very profitable situation for yourself? Quite simply, run a business, own a property, and obtain the best loan possible. Well, let me give you an example of a borrower that once took advantage of this.

A few years ago, one of my previous clients who owned a photography business was looking for new studio space. She asked me for advice, and I explained to her that she could use this owner financing tactic to find a space and actually get paid to work there. She located a 30% occupied two-story office building that was about 20,000 square feet which was actually for sale. With the current income, the property was only worth about $1.2 million. Unfortunately, her financials were not strong enough to acquire the building on her own. Luckily, one of her good friends, a dentist, was looking for a place to rent. As a sidebar, medical professionals, especially dentists and doctors, achieve the highest leverage through many lending sources like SBA. Most of these professionals can achieve 115% financing which covers the entire purchase and working capital for equipment with a 25/25 self-amortizing loan[7].

The office building offered 7,000 square feet for the photographer and 4,000 square feet for the dentist. With the 6,000 square feet currently leased, they were left with 3,000 square feet of additional space to lease up. Together, they occupied 55% of the building which allowed them to qualify for owner occupied financing. They received a 90% LTV plus 15% for working capital at a rate of 5.25% for 25

---

[7] National conventional lenders i.e. Wells Fargo, Bank of America, Regions Bank, etc offers the best SBA programs for Doctors and Dentists.

years from an SBA lender. After obtaining the loan and acquiring the property, they removed the month-to-month tenants, increased all other tenants to the then market rent, reduced the space they occupied to a total 4,000 square feet, and was able to get the property to 100% occupancy with tenants on 3-5 year leases. They did this by hiring a broker that focuses on landlord representation. Because the property fundamentals were now very strong, the new owners were able to sell the property for $2.3 million. This kicked off their investing career. Since that original transaction, they have been involved in a number of owner occupied deals and their net worth continues to grow.

Here's What You Now Know...

1. What an owner occupied loan is and why it's the best loan to obtain
2. How to utilize this loan to have a higher loan to value, longer term, and a lower than average interest rate
3. If you can't do it on your own, partner with someone in the medical field!

YOUR HOMEWORK...

Do you have a business? Of course you do! You invest in real estate! With that, think of ways to use this loan type in order to maximize your next or current investment. Look for vacant properties or near-vacant properties on the market. Visualize the types of tenants that could flourish there. Befriend a landlord representative in your market and ask them to visit the vacant property with you. Is there a way to flip the property in two years to an investor looking to acquire a fully occupied building.

CHAPTER EIGHT

What is a Financing Memorandum and Why Do You Need One?

*W*hen a lender prepares a loan for you, they go through many channels to get it approved. As mentioned in previous chapters, your typical lender will present your property and situation to their credit committee who ultimately makes the final decision to lend on your asset or not. Because of this, lenders need to put their best foot forward. They do this by compiling data into a committee package which includes many data points to support the deal to get it funded. Who do you think the lender cares about more, your property and goals or the bank that they are employed by? Obviously the bank! Because of this, creating the investment package on your own can help put you in a better light and potentially get you a lower rate, longer term, and higher leverage.

A well-read, well-written loan proposal package will help make the lenders' job easy. The less work they do, the quicker your loan will be approved. If you contact the right lenders with enough information, you will be able to convince them that it makes sense to finance your property. You'd want to make sure you tell the best story about the investment, remove the unnecessary expenses so that you can push the value of your property, and speak to the strength of the asset and yourself. A financing memorandum does just that. In this chapter, we will describe what a financing memo entails, why each section is important, and what order your financing package should be in. Remember, you are doing this to obtain a better rate and better terms. Otherwise, you will be leaving this for the lender to decide while also leaving money on the table.

What Does the Financing Memo Entail?

Cover Letter

The first thing you must create is a cover letter. On your cover letter, your job is to make a recommendation for financing based upon your evaluation of the deal, your needs as a borrower, and based on the needs of the lender. Remember, the lender is theoretically investing in the property with you, so they need to be assured that they will have a solid property in their portfolio.

You will need to include a succinct overview of the four main deal elements that we have discussed above and what you are looking to accomplish.

- *The Real Estate*
- *The Market*
- *The Property's Financials*
- *Your Track Record and Financial Strength*

Opening Statement

An opening statement is a brief overview of what you're looking for. It makes the lenders aware that you have a detailed proposal ready for review – here's an example of an opening statement:

"The attached information is in referenced to the strip retail center I

am planning to acquire in Orlando, FL. The site is 2.32 acres with three retail buildings totaling 29,197 sf. containing a 4,000 sf. restaurant space and 25,197 sf. of side shops. The restaurant is leased to Denny's. The total equity will be 25% of the property's value. Value is estimated to be about $11 per sf. or $1.1 million."

- Summary of Loan Terms Requested:
- Amount:
- Interest rate: - i.e., Prime + 1
- Term: (in months)

Make brief comments about yourself as it relates to your experience in real estate

You want to make sure the lender will be comfortable giving you the money you're requesting. They will want to know your background, your personal experience with commercial real estate, your track record and experience in investing in the type of property you're looking to finance, how many properties in your portfolio, your net worth and liquidity today and after the transaction is complete. You also want to include your personal financial statement and any partner that has more than 10% of ownership into your holding company, a full overview of your current portfolio, and make sure to have your personal and business tax returns ready and available upon request.

Make brief comments about the real estate and the market

Your purpose here is to identify any possible concerns, issues or problems if they exist in the real estate market, the property specifically, and if none, to give overall comfort to the lender that the deal is mainstream and issues or special considerations should not

come up later. You want to highlight the strengths of the transaction and the challenges of the deal that may not be understood from the outside looking in. Basically, if you anticipate any surprises, divulge them now. Trust me, you cannot and will not fool the lender.

Describe briefly your underwriting

Describe how you have underwritten property and the loan. Make sure to use the following:

- *Underwriting Property Level Analysis (PLA)*
- *Sources and Uses of Funds – describing what you will do with any funds you will recoup after a refinance*
- *Property Rent Roll – As detailed as possible. Try and obtain each tenant's name and suite/unit/street number, square feet occupied, lease start and end dates, date of original occupancy, monthly base rent (net of sales tax), detailed breakdown of expenses together with any tenant reimbursements, annual rent escalations, and renewal options.*
- *24-60 month Pro forma – A pro forma is a projection that tells a story about what the lender can expect from you managing the property.*
- *3 Years of Operating Statements [monthly Profit and Loss statements work the best]*
- *Property Expense Analysis [if you have CAPEX that you'd like to mention]*
- *Credit information on key tenants*

Property Zoning Report (PZR)

You will never know, but a lender will create their own form of property zoning report in every single transaction they finance. A property zoning report is used to give lenders an overview of what the property is zoned and if the property meets the zoning code. This is an extremely important feature that is due its own chapter, so let's revisit this in Chapter Eight.

Exhibits

Exhibits are pictures that tell a story of the property and market. In your package, location maps, a map detailing the neighborhood and aerial maps are critical and must be included. You can create them easily from Google Earth. Other exhibits that are important to include are, a site plan to show access points, pictures of the property, pictures of the parking lot, pictures of the roof, and ac units.

Additional items that are important to include in your financing request are as follows:

- *Sample Lease*
- *Third Party Reports – appraisals, property conditions reports, Phase I environmental assessments*

If you combine the attached into a strong proposal, you will be able to achieve the lowest rate financing in the shortest amount of time.

Here's What You Now Know about What a Financing Memo is and Why you need one...

1. *What a Financing Memorandum is and why it's important you have one to present when looking for financing*
2. *The items needed to complete a loan proposal and why they are in a certain order*
3. *How everything you've learned in this book can help you create a well written and well organized financing memorandum*

YOUR HOMEWORK...

Put together a sample package and set up a meeting with your lender. This will be great practice for you even if you're not looking for financing today. Create a dialogue about your package and make sure to incorporate questions the lender asks you into your final package. Your goal is to have the answer to most of the lender's questions in your financing memorandum.

CHAPTER NINE

A Property Zoning Report? What is This and Why is It So Important to Have?

*W*hen *lenders give you the "thumbs up" on financing your property and you receive your final approval letter, you may not know this, but some sort of a zoning verification has been completed. A zoning report is not uncommon when obtaining a loan to acquire a property or refinance a current property. Zoning due diligence has become a necessary requisite process in every real estate investment transaction. Lenders, bankers, insurers, and buyers need to minimize their risk and ensure their investment is smart, safe, and profitable. A zoning report allows you to do this.*

Typically, the underwriter performs a basic zoning search and reviews all pertinent codes related to your transaction. They will not tell you anything about the zoning, as they expect you to complete this on your own during due diligence. Not only is having a zoning report important for the lender, but also it's extremely important for the borrower, although most borrowers will never know about it. Having a zoning report is important if you plan to build on adjacent land, extend parking, further develop the building, etc. A zoning report outlines whether a property conforms to, or is in compliance with, its municipality's zoning code.

If your property was developed when an older version of the current building and zoning code was in effect, the property will usually be considered legally nonconforming. In the event that a property becomes legally nonconforming, commonly referred to as "grandfathered," banks and lenders require a certain damage and reconstruction threshold percentage to again minimize the risk to their investment. If a newer version of the ordinance is in place and there is a bad fire or other major damage to the property, many jurisdictions require the property to be rebuilt to the current code. For example, in the Orange County Zoning Code[8], if your property is destroyed, you may not be able to rebuild it. It states:

"A nonconforming building or structure, other than a sign, which is destroyed by any cause or means (including a flood, fire, hurricane, tornado, storm, explosion, riot, or other calamity), ***shall not be replaced****, except in compliance with the regulations of this chapter. A nonconforming building or structure, other than a sign, which is damaged by any cause or means, such that the cost of repair is in excess of seventy-five (75) percent of the assessed value of the building or structure as of January 1 of the calendar year that the building or structure was damaged, as calculated by the Orange County Property Appraiser; or, if applicable, by the Orange County Value Adjustment Board, shall not be repaired, except in compliance with the regulations of this chapter."*

The above clearly states that if your property is destroyed by you or any "Act of God" over 75% of the assessed value, you will have to redevelop the property to the updated standard. A zoning ordinance is the written document describing in detail the permitted uses in each district. The ordinance also details physical requirements for

---

[8] *Municode*, Orange County, FL, 2019, library.municode.com/fl/orange_county/codes/code_of_ordinances?nodeId=ORCOCO_CH38ZO.

developing a property such as minimum lot size, density, setbacks from property lines, building height limits, parking requirements, and landscaping. This could change building heights, setbacks, landscaping, and parking requirements. This can be a significant investment issue and could inevitably cost you thousands, if not millions of dollars. Therefore, it is important to know what the zoning ordinance requires when property damages exceed a certain percentage of the replacement value.

A few years ago, I worked with a borrower who was looking to acquire a single tenant net lease asset with an extremely strong tenant. This property type/ tenant type combination generally commands a very aggressive cap rate. This one in particular was a 5% cap rate. This means that on this purchase of $4 million, the NOI on this property was $200,000. Because the loan constant was much higher than the cap rate, the investor was looking at a negative leverage. What needed to happen was that the investor needed to find a way to increase his income. The listing broker told the investor that the tenant had plans to build an extension of the property on the adjacent parcel – which was included in the sale. The borrower saw this as an excellent opportunity, so he put it under contract. I performed a Property Zoning Report for the borrower on what was currently allowed and what was potentially allowed on the adjacent building. During due diligence, we found out that the current parking was insufficient based on the zoning code and with the expansion, the tenants would definitely require additional parking. Needless to say, because of the parking, the borrower was now aware that the plans to expand may have not been true. After requesting expansion details, and the listing broker coming up short, the borrower cancelled the contract. If we hadn't done the Property Zoning Report for him, he would have more than likely continued with the acquisition making a *grave mistake.*

Another clause in the zoning ordinance that you should be concerned with is considered the discontinuation of a nonconforming use or what's also known as the "go dark" clause. Specifically in single-tenant properties, this clause gives you a period of time allowed for a nonconforming use to remain grandfathered in if the property becomes vacant. In the Orlando, FL Zoning Code[9], it states the following:

*"When a nonconforming use has been discontinued for any reason for a period of **six months**, all subsequent uses shall revert to those permitted by this Chapter."*

The above means that if your property is nonconforming and becomes vacant for a period of six months, you will have to convert your property to the conforming status of the zoning ordinance. With this said, if you are acquiring a property, it is extremely important to understand that if the zoning ordinance has changed since the time the building was developed.

Why is Zoning Important to You?

Banks and other financial institutions generally require a property to be in compliance with zoning ordinances before they will issue a loan. With zoning codes ever-changing, a zoning report provides confidence to the lender and investors that the current and future use of the property will comply with local laws. Also, your investment and hard-earned cash is at risk. Understanding if your property is legally nonconforming will help you with your offer, help you with your future plans as it relates to the investment, and will allow you

---

[9] *Municode*, City of Orlando, 2019, library.municode.com/fl/orlando/codes/code_of_ordinances?nodeId=TITIICICO_CH58ZODIUS.

to remain less at risk than you would have otherwise been.

Here's What You Now Know about a Property Zoning Report and Why it's important for you to Have One...

1. What is a Property Zoning Report?
2. Why the nonconforming language in the zoning ordinance is vitally important for you to know and understand
3. What you need to do in order to ensure you are investing in the right property with the right goal in mind

YOUR HOMEWORK...

Check online for your property's zoning classification. Usually, this is on the property appraiser's website. Once you have the classification, locate your zoning ordinance. Check the date the zoning ordinance was last updated. Is your property older than the last date the zoning ordinance was updated? Review your parking current parking against the zoning code. Also compare your building and density requirements, go dark, and your nonconforming language. You can use this information to adjust your plans accordingly and possibly ensure that your CAPEX reserves are healthy just in case. Being safe is always better than being sorry.

CHAPTER TEN

This Process Seems Very Complicated and Overwhelming. Can Someone Do This For Me?

In the eight years I've been directly involved in commercial real estate finance, I've done many lectures and had numerous discussions with potential buyers and borrowers. Mostly, I'm asked, "Where do I go to learn all this information? What documents do I need to present to the lender in order to maximize this investment? How will everything be viewed by the credit committee?" Let's recap to ensure you are fully aware of how to do this.

Remember, you want to make sure that you package your information so that it's brain dead simple to understand from the lenders' point of view. Keep in mind; lenders do not like to work on deals that they would consider challenging, as their focus is usually on properties and transactions that take the least amount of time and work. That said, the easier you make the process and the easier it will be for the lender, the higher the chances are that you will get your transaction to the finish line.

To reiterate, your loan request needs to include an overview and executive summary describing who you are and what type of loan terms you're interested in. You want to put together a short bio on yourself and partners and want to show the lender that you have experience in real estate. This doesn't mean that you need to have a ton of experience in product acquisition. The idea here is that you want to help the lender become comfortable in your ability to maintain the property and keep their investment profitable.

Another thing that you want to include in your package is a PLA, or Property Level Analysis, which includes the financial analysis and rent roll of the property. Like I mentioned, you need to understand how to determine an NOI, how to remove one time expenses or CAPEX line items, and include solid projections for the next 24 to 60 months. This is the pro forma projection that describes what you intend to happen while managing the property. Apart from the PLA, you want to submit a sample lease. If you own or are acquiring a multi-tenant retail building, you want to show them a sample lease from one or two of the tenants.

If you have any third-party reports, such as appraisals, Phase I environmental analysis and reports, you want to supply those to the lenders. You also would want to provide details on any title issues or any survey issues that you have knowledge of. One thing that most people don't think about is the potential zoning issue that could incur while acquiring a property.

There are things that take place behind closed doors, and lenders will do this report and analysis. Just recently, this happened to one of the transactions I was working on, where there was what's called a shared easement that actually was not recorded in the county.

If it's correctly put together, lenders will appreciate that much more than if you give them a bunch of tax returns that's not in order. You want to make sure that you have your tax returns and your *financials, your personal financial story, easily legible so that the lender can understand it. If you have a multifamily asset, have your rent roll, pictures of the property, and profit and loss statement available.*

By compiling these documents together in a package, not only will it make things easier for yourself, but also for the lender and allow the process to go much smoother.

It's Still Too Overwhelming. Can Someone Do This for Me?

After looking over the above and you still feel overwhelmed, don't fret! You can have everything mentioned in this book completed for you by a well-informed capital advisor who specializes in commercial real estate investment property. A commercial real estate capital markets advisor can be confused with a commercial mortgage broker, but the two are dramatically different. A commercial mortgage broker will connect you with a lender, maybe negotiate the transaction on your behalf, and help you close the transaction. A capital markets advisor does the job of a mortgage broker on steroids! A capital markets advisor will create your financing request package, help to determine if you should refinance or sell, provide you with numerous options to increase your value and recoup your value, they hold your hand throughout the process, they get to know and understand your goals, and have access to theoretically unlimited sources of capital ranging from wholesale bank rates and life insurance company financing to commercial mortgage backed securities and government-sponsored programs to tailor a mortgage program to your unique needs.

A capital markets advisor will package all the information that I've laid out in this book to provide a seamless process for you. All you would need to do is provide the information, and everything else will be done for you again and again, practically on auto-pilot.

Now, what's the best way that we can work together?

Although I'm not a capital markets advisor any longer, there is no risk in talking to me about your investment and capital needs, specifically if you own or are looking to own a multifamily property. For other property types, I have many connections in the marketplace. Whether you'd want to sell your property, refinance your property, or acquire a property, let me know. I can put you in touch with a trusted advisor to help you get the appropriate financing and price you deserve and need.

If you're interested in learning about how I can help you finance your multifamily asset, send me a quick email. I am more than happy helping you quickly secure a loan to acquire a new investment or refinance your existing asset, now and in the future.

So what's next?

The first thing that I would recommend you do is to email me directly at CREBook2019@gmail.com. In the subject line, add "Money-Saving Multifamily Investment Maximizer Strategy Session". This will help me sift through the junk mail. Then just drop me a line and let's schedule a time to talk about your plans and your goals as it relates to either using debt to acquiring your next multifamily investment property or refinancing your current multifamily asset.

It's been a pleasure to be able to share with you some of my experience and hope you found it helpful.

APPENDIX

Typical Loan Timing

1. **Getting the Loan Started** Day 1

   <u>Information to start loan process:</u>
   Current Rent Roll
   Operating Income Statements for last three years
   Executed Purchase Contract (if acquiring the property)
   Executed Escrow Instructions
   Preliminary Title Report
   Signed Application with deposit check
   Executed LOI for Lender
   (The loan process does not start without this information)

2. **Third Party Reports/Borrower Information** Day 1-30

   <u>Required Borrower information:</u>
   Borrower must supply the following prior to the issuance of a commitment;
   Borrower's last three years of tax returns (does not apply if you are applying for a GSE loan)
   Borrower's current financial statements
   Borrower's schedule of real estate owned
   Borrower's real estate experience resume
   Entity Documents (LLC, LLP, Trust, etc...)
   <u>The Appraisal:</u>
   Appraiser starts initial research
   Appraiser contacts listing agent to get access to property
   Appraiser walks property with property manager/listing agent
   Appraisal is finalized
   <u>Environmental Report</u>
   <u>Structural Report</u>
   <u>Termite Report</u>

3. **Final Underwriting/Commitment** Day 21-45

   <u>Final Underwriting (final underwriting does not start without all information submitted):</u>

Final underwriting takes place once all borrower, property and third party reports are received
Final underwriting takes two to three weeks
The Commitment:
Once the a commitment is issued and signed, Loan Documents are started
Depending on the lender, docs take two to seven working days to complete

4. **Closing**   **Day 45-60**

Closing:
Docs are signed and returned to escrow
Once all escrow instructions are satisfied the loan is prepared to fund and close
Typically loans fund one day and close the next

Portfolio Loans will typically close between 30-45 days
Conduit/ GSE Loans will typically close in the 60 day range

FIVE KEYS TO UNDERWRITING

Improvements:
- Quality of construction
- Parking ratio
- Leasing depths
- Configuration
- Obsolescence

Location:
- Feasibility
- Accessibility to site
- Traffic count (retail)
- Highest and Best Use
- Area demographics

Sponsorship:
- Experience in owning comparable properties
- Financials with emphasis on liquidity and net worth
- Management capability
- Equity contribution (20%+)

Nature and Status of Leasing:
- Occupancy
- Rollover exposure
- Market rents?
- Market vacancy
- Credit of tenants
- Sales PSF (retail)

Loan Characteristics:
- Loan To Value

- *Debt Coverage Ratio*
- *Debt Yield*
- *Loan PSF*
- *Capitalization Rate*

Glossary

Definitions pertaining to NOI –

1. *Base Rent* - The base rent is the initial rent, and depending on the lease provisions it may change over the term of the lease.
2. *Effective Rent* - The actual rental rate that the landlord achieves after deducting the concession value from the base rental rate a tenant pays
3. *Loss to lease* - Potential Market Rent minus Scheduled Base Rental Revenue
4. *Vacancy Factor* - a measurement of gross rental income loss due to vacancy and non-collection of rent.
5. *Operating Expenses* - an expense required for the day-to-day functioning of a business
6. *Capital Expenditures* - an expense that a business incurs to create a benefit in the future
7. *Rent Roll* - the total income arising from rented property
8. *Reserves and Replacements* - an account set aside by an individual or business to meet any unexpected costs that may arise in the future as well as the future costs of upkeep
9. *Tenant Improvement* - The tenant improvement allowance is the amount a landlord is willing to spend so that the tenant can retrofit or renovate the office space.
10. *CAM* - A CAM (common area maintenance) charge is an additional rent, charged on top of base rent, and is mainly composed of maintenance fees for work performed on the common area of a property.
11. *Expense Stop* - An expense stop is a tool used by landlords to limit their exposure to operating costs, and as such helps to maintain predictable operating expenses over the term of a lease.
12. *Trailing Income* - Typically trailing twelve months P&Ls are generated to show either the most recent twelve months of a

company's trading or to show the last twelve months of its trading before a certain date

Definitions pertaining to Debt –

1. *Loan to Value* – LTV – the ratio of the first mortgage lien as a percentage of the total appraised value of real property
2. *Debt Coverage Ratio* - A DSCR greater than 1 means the entity – whether a person, company or government – has sufficient income to pay its current debt obligations. A DSCR less than 1 means it does not. NOI/Annual Debt Service
3. *Amortization* - The paying off of debt with a fixed repayment schedule in regular installments over a period of time
4. *Interest Only* - The borrower pays only the interest on the principal balance, with the principal balance unchanged
5. *Balloon* - a mortgage which does not fully amortize over the term of the note, thus leaving a balance due at maturity
6. *Loan Terms* - how long the loan will exist
7. *Loan to Cost* - A ratio used in commercial real estate construction to compare the amount of the loan used to finance a project to the cost to build the project.
8. *CMBS* - A type of asset-backed security that is secured by a commercial mortgage or collection of commercial mortgages
9. *Taking paper back* – Seller carry or seller financing - Seller financing is defined as a loan provided by the seller of a home to the purchaser.
10. *Self-Liquidating* – a loan that amortization matches its maturity ie. 30/30 in the case of Fannie Mae
11. *Recourse* – personal guarantee of the borrower
12. *Non-Recourse* – no personal guarantees need to be made by the borrower
13. *Leverage* – debt and/or equity contribution within a capital stack

14. _Debt Yield_ – lender's cash on cash – NOI/Principal Loan Amount
15. _Loan Balance_ – principal amount of the loan
16. _Principal Reduction_ – paying an amount over the monthly or annual debt service will be applied to the principal loan balance
17. _Defeasance_ - allows the borrower to exchange another cash flowing asset for the original collateral for the loan to avoid large PPP fees
18. _Yield Maintenance_ - a prepayment premium that allows investors to attain the same yield as if the borrower made all scheduled mortgage payments until maturity
19. _Pre-payment Penalty_ – penalty for prepaying the debt prior to the end of the loan term
20. _Loan Constant_ – Mortgage Cap Rate – only applicable to mortgages with fix rate loans - annual debt/original loan principal (true cost of borrowing)

Definitions Pertaining to Leases and Lease Clauses

1. _Gross Lease_ - The tenant pays a flat rental amount, and the landlord pays for all property charges regularly incurred by the ownership.
2. _NNN Lease_ – a lease in which the lessee assumes responsibility for all expenses associated with the property is CAM. Taxes, and Insurance
3. _Percentage Rent_ - A percentage lease is a lease where the rental is based on a percentage of the monthly or annual gross sales made on the premises, usually coupled with a base rent.
4. _Escalators_ - rent can increase by a specified amount each period
5. _Kick out clause_ - also known as a "Cancellation Clause" - A landlord can evict a tenant, or a tenant may vacate the space after a certain period of time has passed, if certain needs or thresholds are not met.

Other Terminology –

1. *Spread* – *portion of the interest rate that the lender changes based on perceived risk of the asset*
2. *Positive Leverage* – *leverage that helps increases the returns of the borrower (mortgage constant is higher than cap rate)*
3. *Negative Leverage* – *leverage that decreases the returns of the borrower (mortgage constant is lower than cap rate)*
4. *Equity Build-up* – *as you pay down the principal balance of mortgage, equity is increased*
5. *Absorption* - *The rate at which available properties or units are sold in a specific real estate market during a given time period*
6. *Rent to sales ratio* – *measures affordability of commercial space. Annual Rent divided by Annual EBITA or total sales (2.5+ is good for NN/NNN property)*
7. *Pro forma* – *future projections of a property's operation*
8. *Sweat Equity* - *an interest or increased value in a property earned from labor toward upkeep or restoration*

TESTIMONIALS

"You have been great. You can use me as a reference anytime and I will send you business whenever I can. As a 20 plus year Wall Street headhunter for the top banks in the world, I can attest to your knowledge and professionalism. Thank you for everything."
Paul Sorbera,
Alliance Consulting

"I wanted to drop you a note to thank you for all your help with our transaction. The mortgage process was smooth, and your service level was excellent. We will definitely look to work with you again in the future."
Pompi Malik,
Multifamily Owner

"One of the worst things you could do is not use Charles for financing. Not only is he a professional and knows what he's doing, but he has his fingers on the pulse of the marketplace and gets deals done. This year we've closed almost $20,000,000 with Charles and we plan to at least double that next year. The resources that he offers are unparalleled in the market, and Charles uses them to ensure my clients achieve the best financing out there."
Colin Colby,
Marcus & Millichap Real Estate Investment Services

www.ingramcontent.com/pod-product-compliance
Lightning Source LLC
Chambersburg PA
CBHW022113170526
45157CB00004B/1611